Dog Groups

Working Group

by Julie Murray

Dash!
LEVELED READERS
An Imprint of Abdo Zoom • abdobooks.com

Level 1 – Beginning
Short and simple sentences with familiar words or patterns for children who are beginning to understand how letters and sounds go together.

Level 2 – Emerging
Longer words and sentences with more complex language patterns for readers who are practicing common words and letter sounds.

Level 3 – Transitional
More developed language and vocabulary for readers who are becoming more independent.

abdobooks.com

Published by Abdo Zoom, a division of ABDO, PO Box 398166, Minneapolis, Minnesota 55439.
Copyright © 2024 by Abdo Consulting Group, Inc. International copyrights reserved in all countries.
No part of this book may be reproduced in any form without written permission from the publisher.
Dash!™ is a trademark and logo of Abdo Zoom.

Printed in the United States of America, North Mankato, Minnesota.
102023
012024

Photo Credits: Getty Images, Shutterstock
Production Contributors: Jennie Forsberg, Grace Hansen
Design Contributors: Candice Keimig, Neil Klinepier

Library of Congress Control Number: 2023938006

Publisher's Cataloging in Publication Data

Names: Murray, Julie, author.
Title: Working group / by Julie Murray
Description: Minneapolis, Minnesota : Abdo Zoom, 2024 | Series: Dog groups | Includes online resources and index.
Identifiers: ISBN 9781098284077 (lib. bdg.) | ISBN 9781098284794 (eBook) | ISBN 9781098285159 (Read-to-Me eBook)
Subjects: LCSH: Working dogs--Juvenile literature. | Dog breeds--Juvenile literature. | Dogs--Juvenile literature. | Dogs--Behavior--Juvenile literature.
Classification: DDC 636.73--dc23

Table of Contents

Working Group

There are more than 30 dog **breeds** in the Working Group according to the American Kennel Club (AKC).

Portuguese Water Dog

Dogs in this group were **bred** to help humans. They are good at many jobs!

German
Pinscher

Siberian
Husky

Some make good guard dogs. Others can pull sleds or rescue people.

Characteristics

Working dogs are medium to large in size. Some are known as "gentle giants."

WORKING
GROUP
WORKING
GROUP

They are strong dogs and tireless workers. Some are happy to work all day long!
Alaskan Malamute

14

Working dogs are smart and loyal. They are easy to train.

They are **courageous** too!
They will protect their owners
without **hesitation**.

16

Boxer

Working dogs are independent. Some may stray if they are not **contained**.

Many working dogs can be good pets. But they should be cared for by experienced owners.

21

More Working Breeds

Glossary

bred – developed over time for a certain purpose.

breed – a particular type of animal.

contained – controlled or kept within certain limits.

courageous – brave.

hesitation – the action of stopping or pausing.

Index

Online Resources

To learn more about the Working Group, please visit **abdobooklinks.com** or scan this QR code. These links are routinely monitored and updated to provide the most current information available.